PAYING WITHOUT MONEY

MONEY

Patricia Armentrout

The Rourke Press, Inc.
Vero Beach, Florida 32964

PHOTO CREDITS
© Armentrout: Cover, Title, pgs. 8, 15; © Corel Corporation: pgs. 7, 10, 12; © East Coast Studios: pgs. 17, 18, 21;
© Evon Thornton: pg. 4; © Oscar C. Williams: pg. 13

ACKNOWLEDGMENTS
The author acknowledges David Armentrout for his contribution in writing this book.

Library of Congress Cataloging-in-Publication Data

Armentrout, Patricia, 1960 -
Paying without money / by Patricia Armentrout
p. cm. — (Money)
Includes index.
Summary: Discusses different ways people have paid for things throughout history, including barter, cash, credit cards, and checks.
ISBN 1-57103-121-9
1. Money—Juvenile literature. 2. Checks—Juvenile literature. 3. Credit cards—Juvenile literature. 4. Debit cards—Juvenile literature. 5. Travelers' checks—Juvenile literature. 6. Automated tellers—Juvenile literature. [1. Money. 2. Finance, personal.]
I. Title II. Series: Armentrout, Patricia, 1960 - Money.
HG221.5.A697 1996
332.7'6—dc20 96–4568
CIP
AC

Printed in the USA

TABLE OF CONTENTS

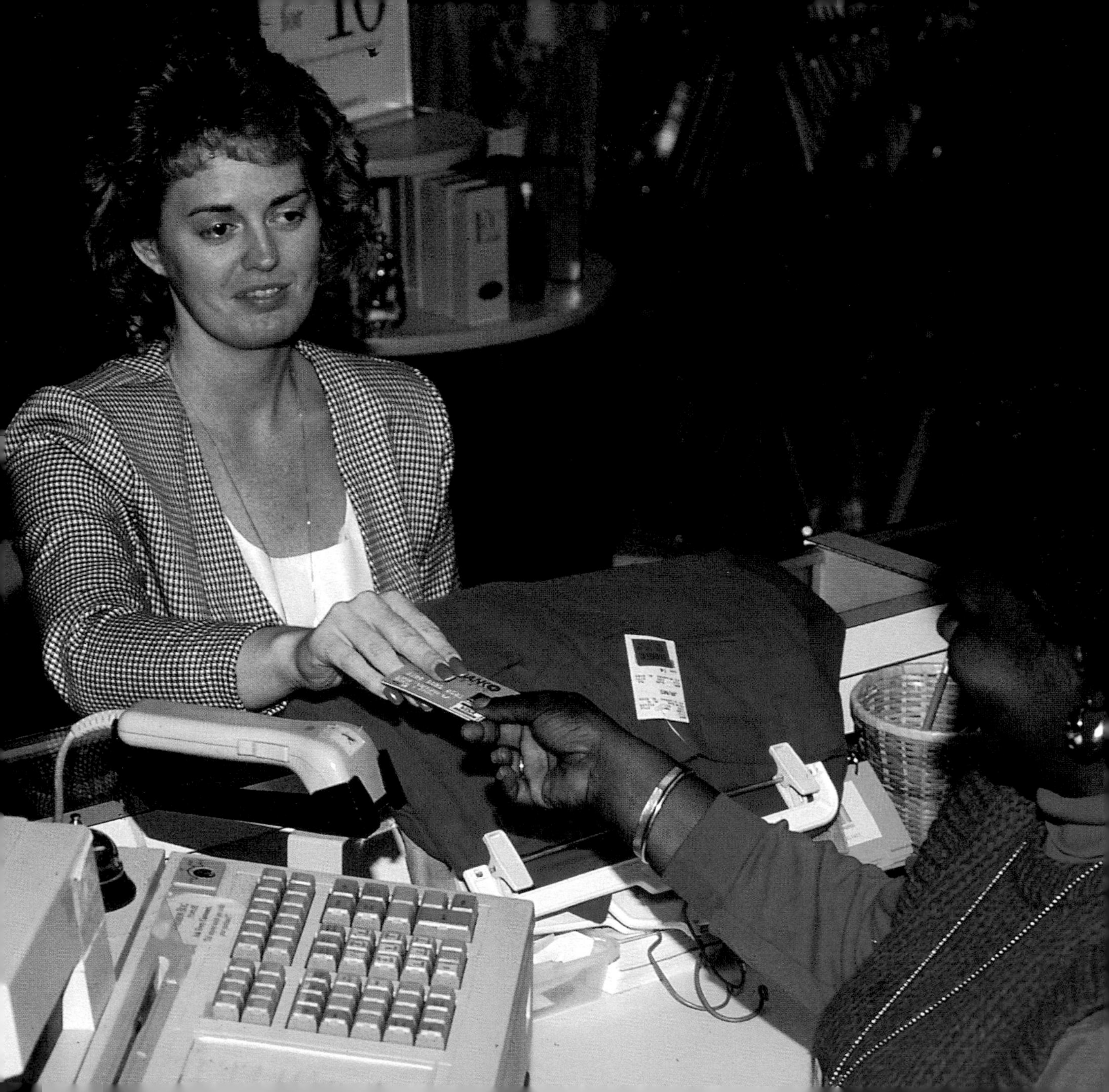

GOODS TRADED FOR GOODS

Paying without money is a very old practice. Long ago, before money was used, people traded things back and forth to get what they needed. People actually paid for goods with other goods.

Today people no longer need to trade goods and services. People can choose different ways to pay for things. Cash, **credit** (KRED it) cards, and checks are just a few forms of payment used worldwide.

Many businesses accept credit cards as payment

BANKS AND MONEY

A bank is a business that takes care of money. Instead of keeping money in a home or business, most people **deposit** (de POZ it) money in a bank.

People deposit money in checking and savings **accounts** (uh KOUNTS). Credit accounts are also available at banks. Most banks offer special services like loaning large amounts of money for a car or a house. They also sell travelers' checks and exchange foreign money.

Banks offer information and services for saving and investing money

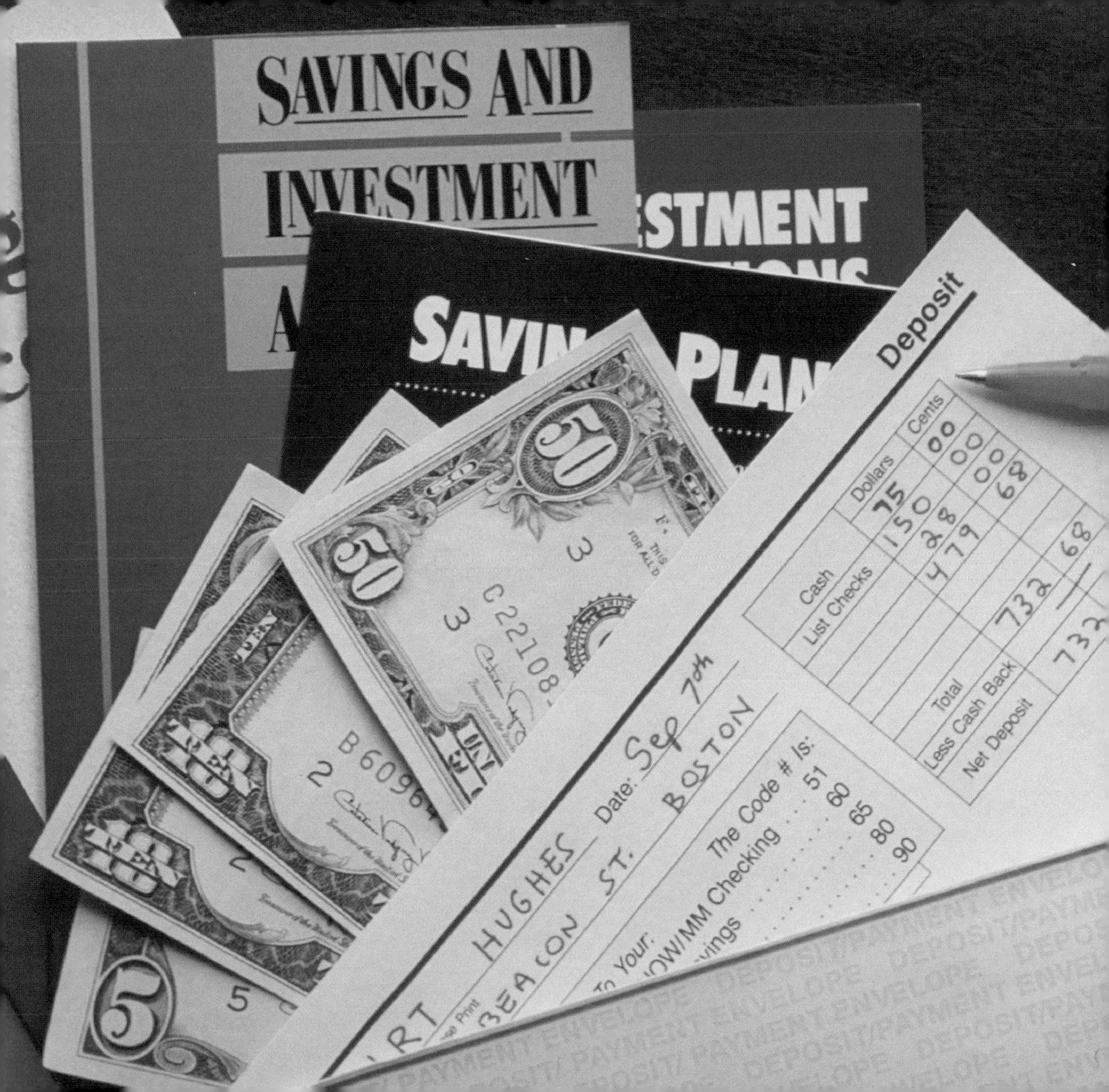
SAVINGS AND
INVESTMENT
ESTMENT
Deposit
Dollars
Cents
Cash
List Checks
75 00
150 00
28 00
479 68
Total
Less Cash Back
Net Deposit
732 68
HUGHES
Date: Sep 7th
BEACON ST. BOSTON
The Code # Is:
DEPOSIT/PAYMENT ENVELOPE

Oct. 12
19 95
1639
$
Dollars

CHECKS

Checks are used in place of cash. To use checks, you need to deposit money into a checking account at a bank. The money deposited is given an account number.

Checks issued by a bank are just pieces of paper with an account number printed on them. The names and addresses of both the bank and account holder are also printed on the checks.

A check is not worth anything until the account holder fills in a payment amount and signs the check.

A signed check allows the bank to release money from your checking account

MIDDLESEX-ESSEX, MA
PM
JUL 27
1993

ACCELERATED PAIN RELIEF CENTER
DR. PETER FOWLER
201 ANDOVER ST.
PEABODY, MA 01960

New England Telephone
NYNEX Company

CREDIT LINE
$5,000

CASH OR CREDIT AVAILABLE
$4,042.25

DAYS IN CYCLE

CLOSING DATE
07/16/93

MINIMUM PAYMENT

JULY 1993 STAT

BROOKLYN PAR
WATERTOWN
BROOKLYN PAR

PAY TO THE

NEW EN

PAYING BILLS

Mailing an envelope filled with cash is a bad idea. There is always a chance the envelope could get lost. Most people pay their bills with checks because it is a safe way to pay.

Items bought from some stores can also be paid for by check. The person writing the check fills in the purchase price and signs the check. The store sends the check to the bank. The bank takes money from the person's checking account and uses it to pay the store.

Paying by check is a way to buy things or pay bills without handling cash.

Most people pay bills with a check and then record the check amount in a check register

Drivers can easily spot automatic teller machines (ATMs) outside buildings

Instead of using money, this woman trades the dolls she makes for food and clothing

DEBIT CARDS

Debit cards work a lot like cash, but cash never changes hands.

Banks give small plastic debit cards to people who have checking accounts. The account holder presents the debit card to the cashier when buying something. The purchase price is deducted from the cardholders checking account.

The use of debit cards has become popular with checking account holders because they no longer need to fill out a check to make a purchase.

Some gas stations make it easy to pay at the pump by accepting debit and credit cards

TURN OFF ENGINE NO SMOKING

BUY NOW AND PAY LATER

Buying something today and paying for it later is called "buying on credit." Many companies and banks offer credit to people.

Most things that people buy on credit cost a lot of money. Houses, cars, boats, furniture, and less expensive items like clothing can be bought on credit.

Banks and credit companies offer credit because they make money from people who use credit cards. The credit companies charge a fee called **interest** (IN trest) to anyone who buys now but pays later.

A loan from a bank to buy a house is a form of credit

Sale
OPUS
ONE
REALTY
Mary Evelyn Bennett
459-9999

Tea
COFFEE
AMERICAN EXPRESS
VISA

CREDIT CARDS

A credit card is a small plastic card that is used to buy on credit. A person presents the card to a cashier for payment. The credit card company agrees to pay the store for the purchase and bills the cardholder later.

A few weeks later the cardholder receives a bill from the credit company. The cardholder has actually borrowed money for a period of time and needs to pay interest on the loan. Interest can be thought of as "the price of borrowing money."

Credit cards are used to purchase everything from clothes to things for your home

TRAVELERS' CHECKS

Travelers' checks can be purchased from banks and are accepted worldwide as cash. The checks are guaranteed to be replaced if lost or stolen. Many people take them when going out of the country or when traveling with large sums of money.

To ensure that the person who purchased the checks is the same one spending them, banks require two signatures: one on each check at the time they are issued, and a second signature when a check is used to make a purchase.

A twenty dollar travelers' check represents the same value as a twenty dollar bill

TWENTY U. S. DOLLARS
102 2592 935 783
8000-0010
20
DATE
SIGNATURE
$20
ISSUER PAY THIS CHEQUE TO
OR ORDER IN THE ABOVE AMOUNT IN ACCORDANCE WITH TERMS ON REVERSE
VISA
TRAVELERS CHEQUE
ISSUER:
Interpayment Services Ltd.,
LONDON, ENGLAND
CHAIRMAN
COUNTERSIGN HERE IN PRESENCE OF PERSON CASHING
8000001031 102592 935783752
OF AMERICA
20
E52900793C

MONEY AND TECHNOLOGY

New **technology** (tek NAHL uh jee) offers people easy ways to deposit, withdraw, and transfer money.

The automated teller machine (ATM) allows people to deposit and withdraw cash without the help of a bank employee. Some banks allow customers to pay bills by transferring money from their accounts to businesses, using buttons on a touch-tone telephone.

Faster, easier methods of transferring money are the way of the future.

Glossary

accounts (uh KOUNTS) — deposits of money in a bank

credit (KRED it) — a loan of money to be paid back over a period of time

deposit (de POZ it) — to put money in a bank for safekeeping

interest (IN trest) — a charge for borrowing money

technology (tck NAHL uh jee) — a science used to improve the things people do and use every day

INDEX